ISBN-13: 978-1517132675

ISBN-10: 1517132673

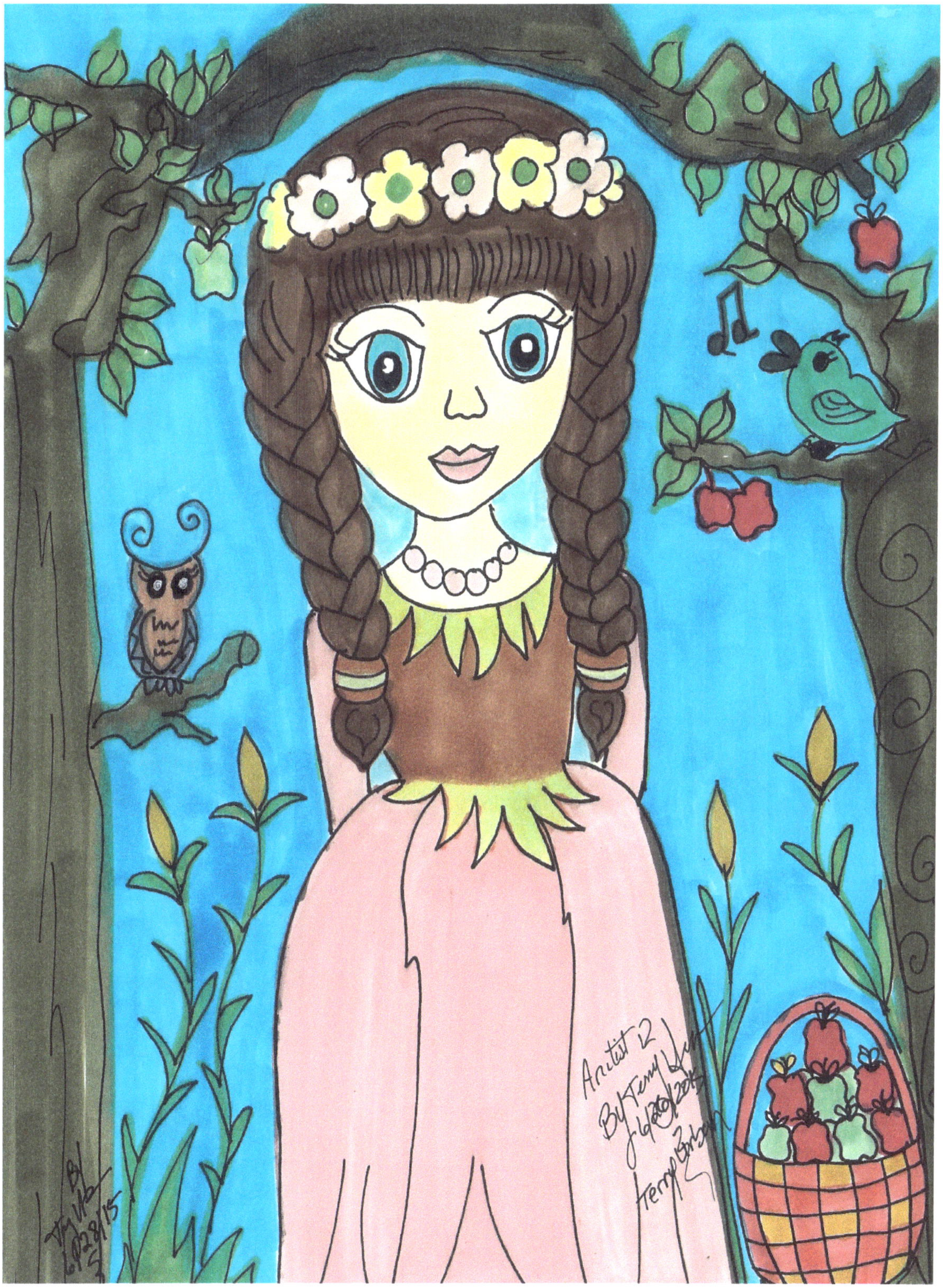
Artist 12

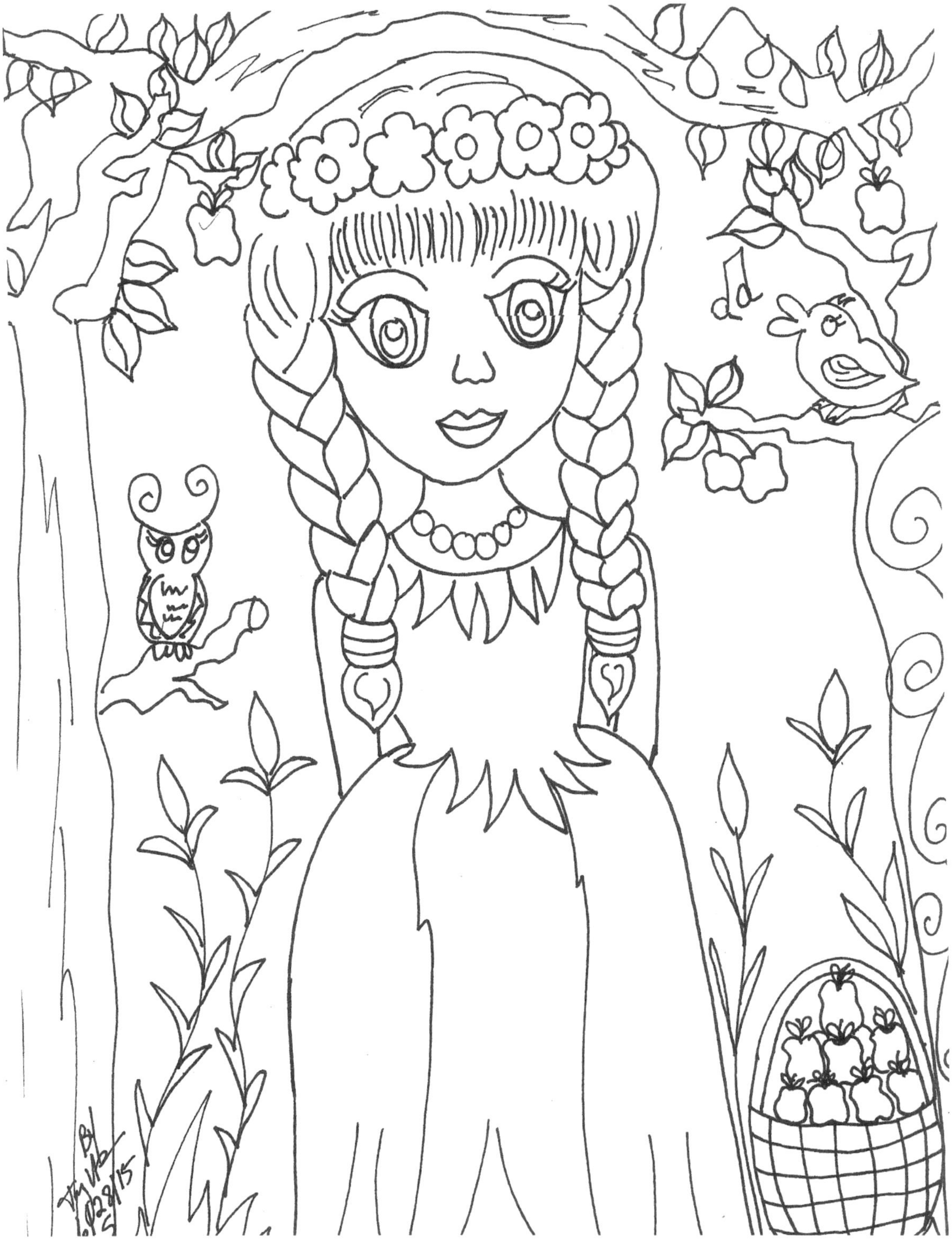

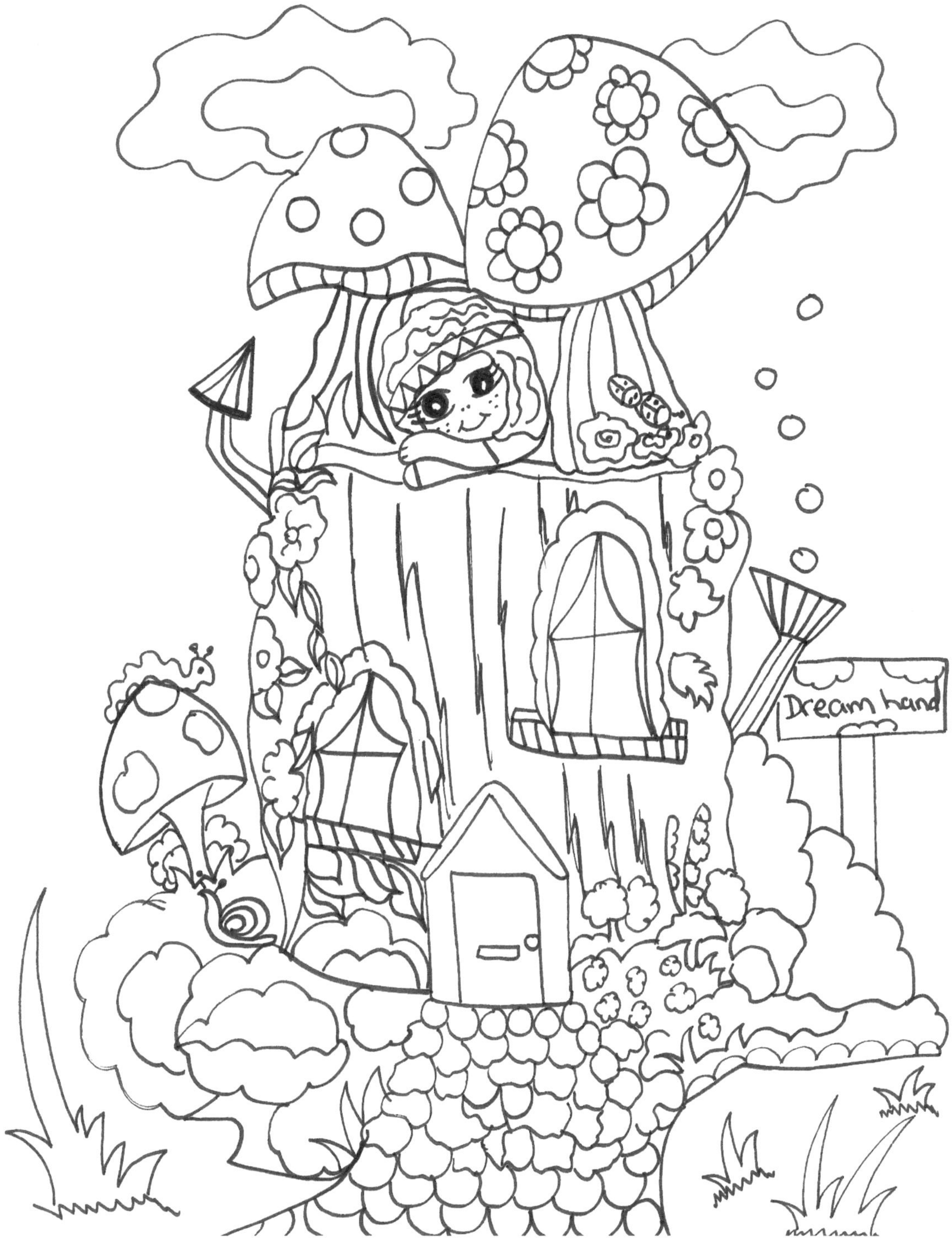
Dream land

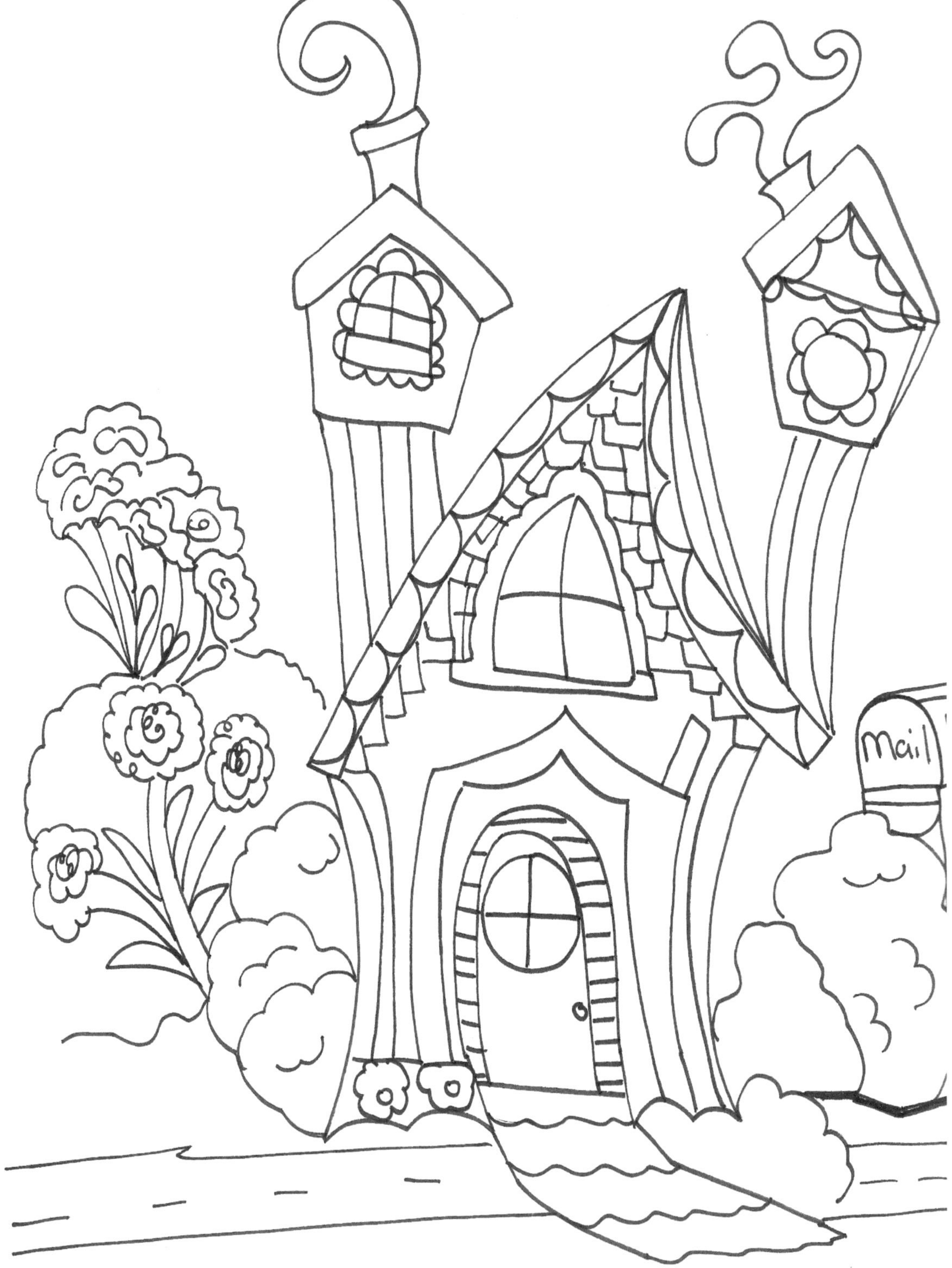
Mail

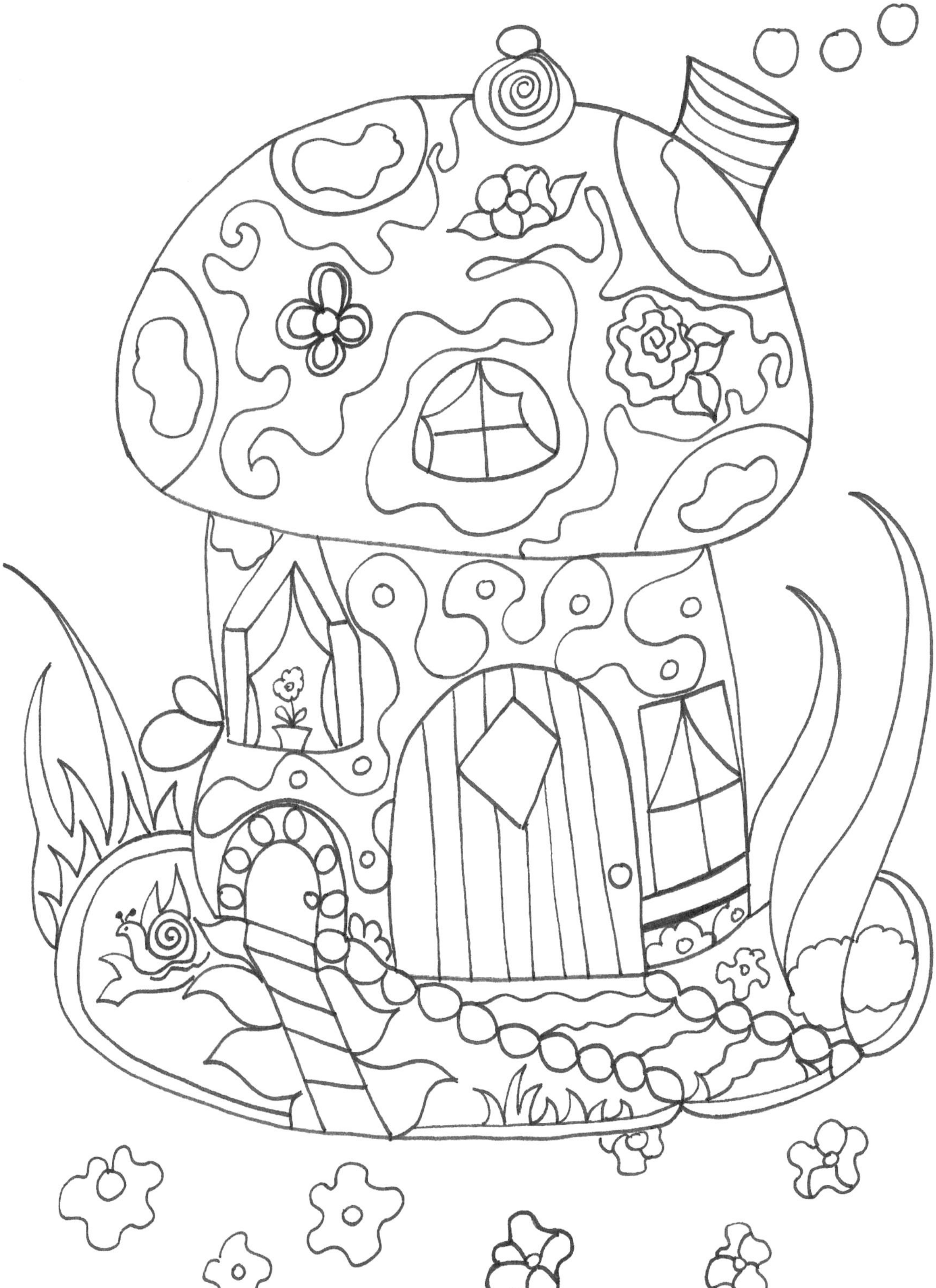

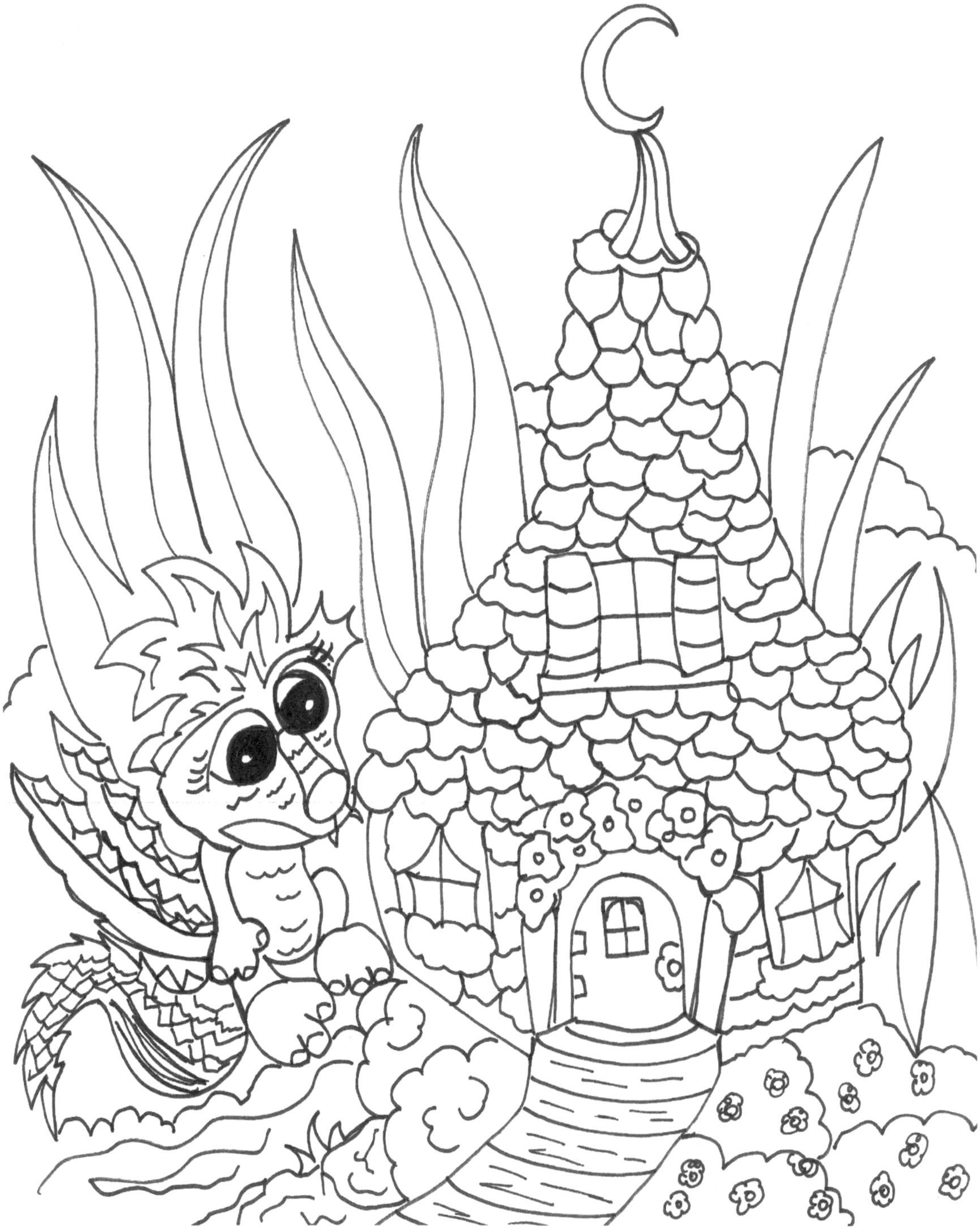

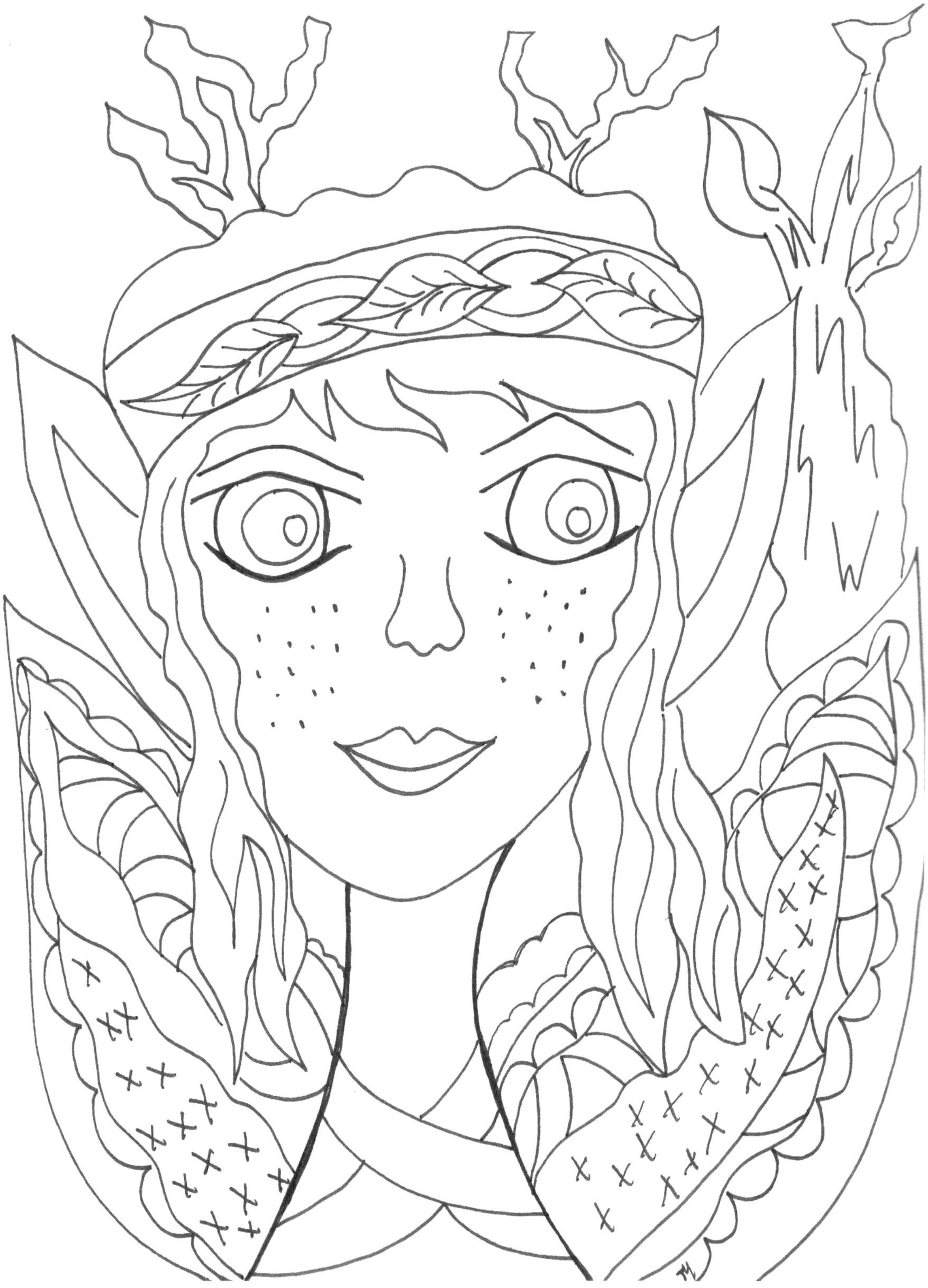

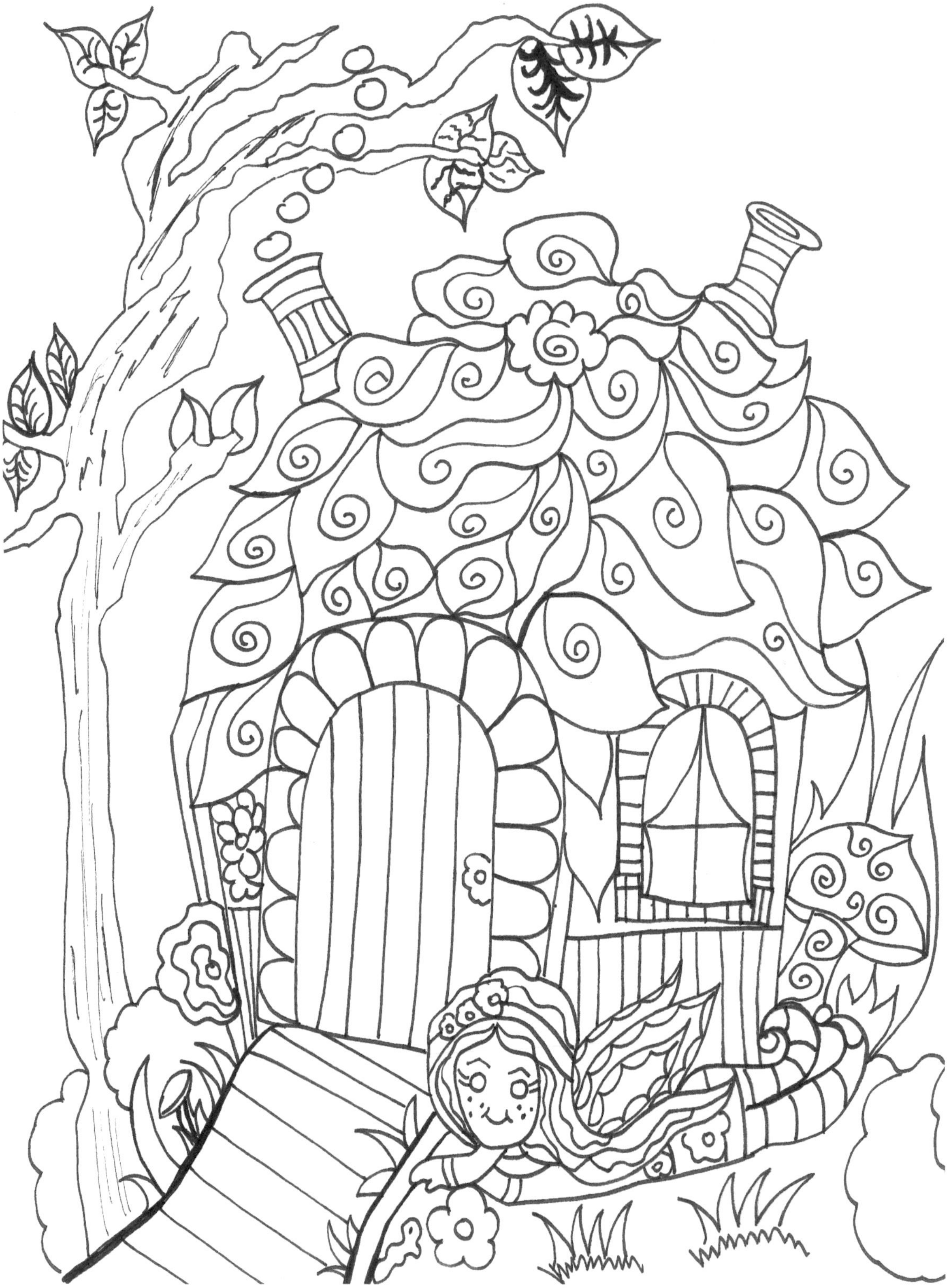

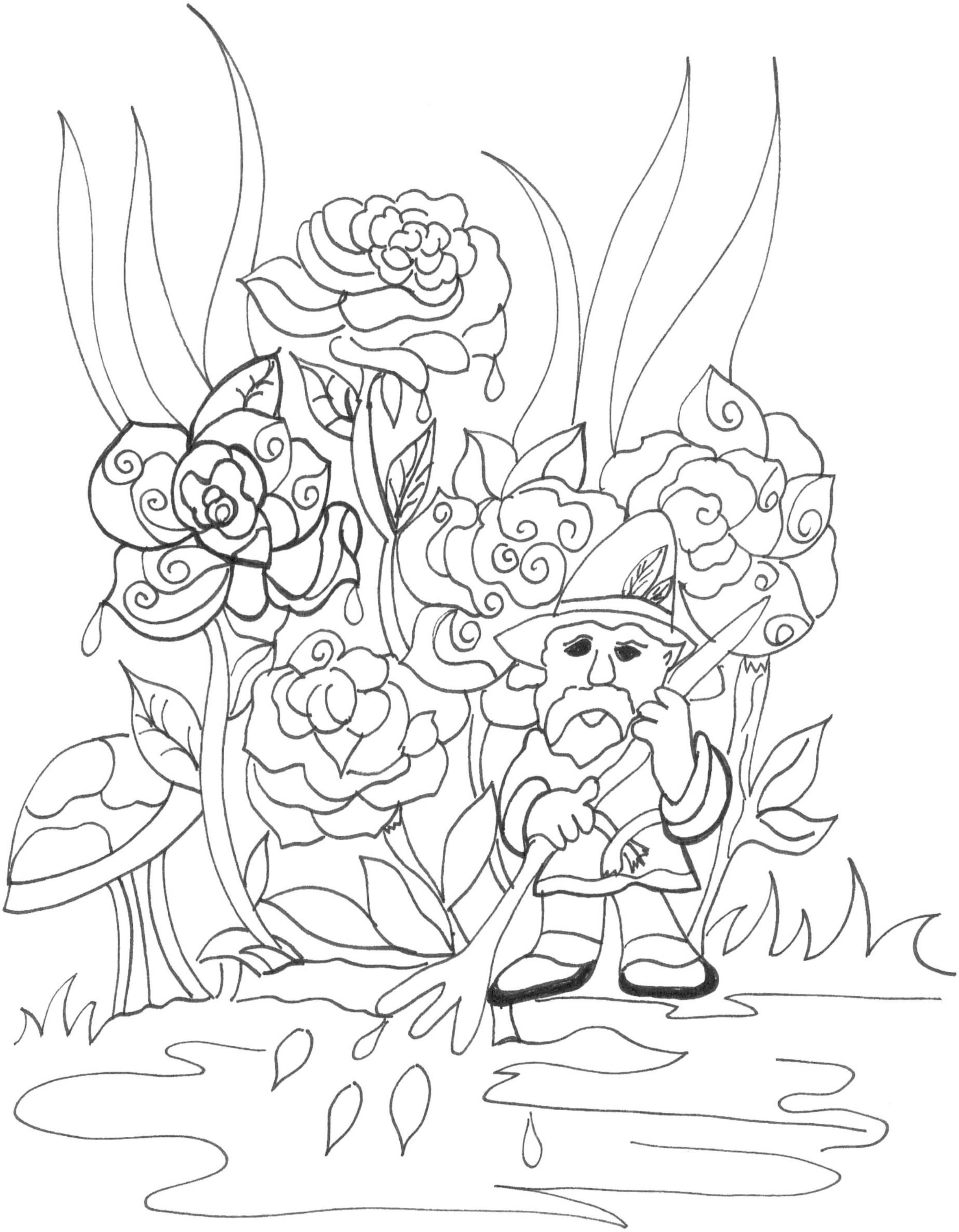

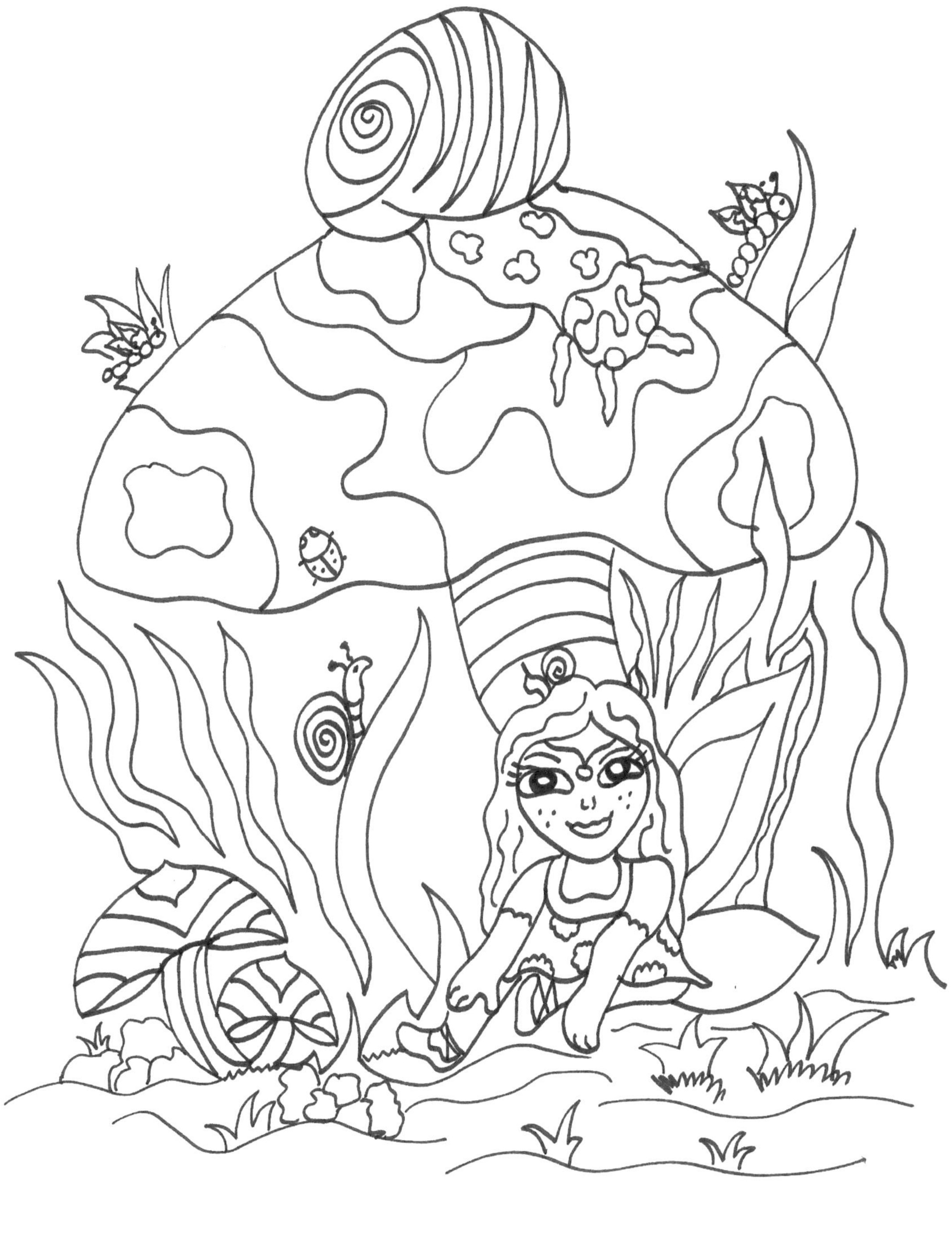

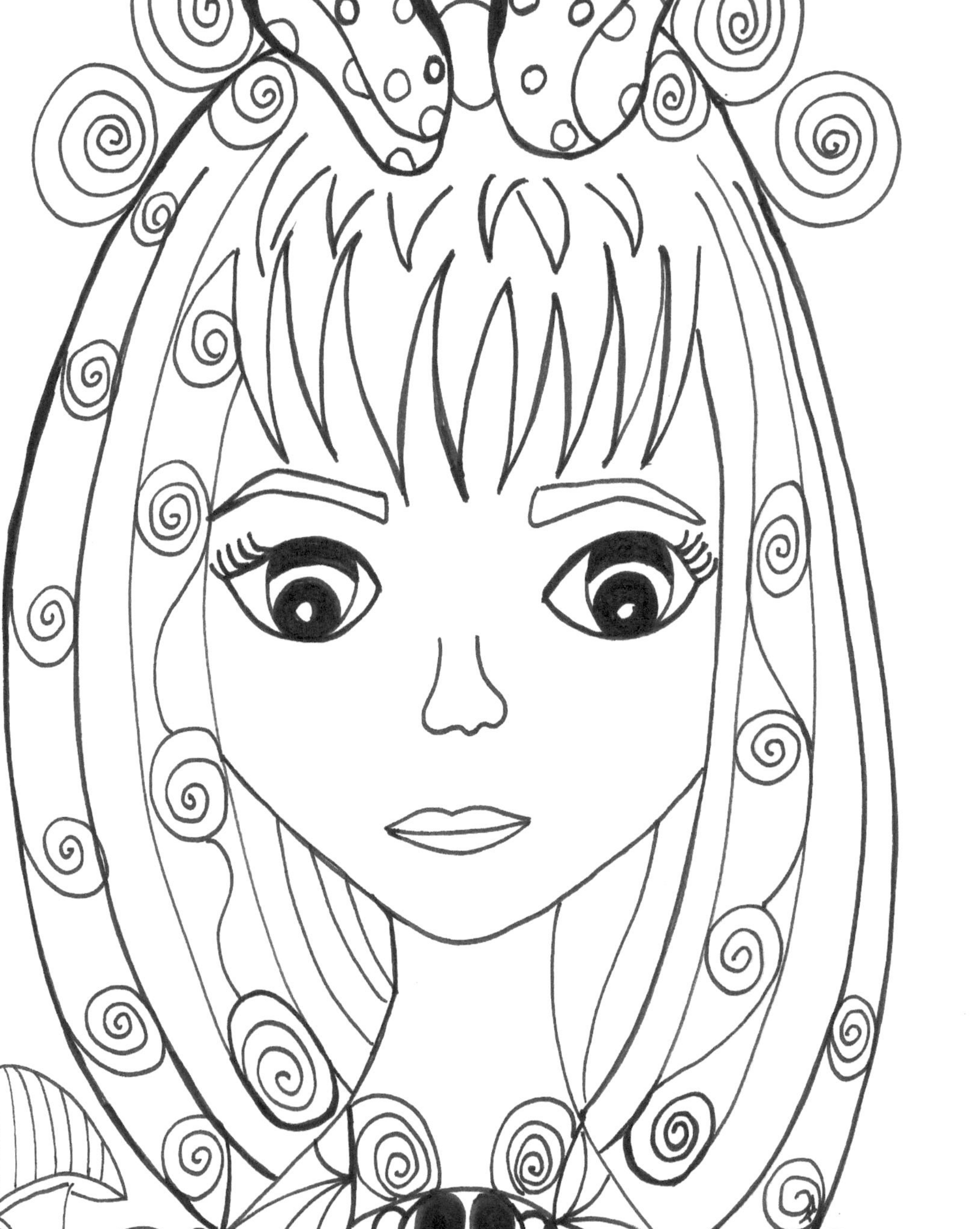
© By Terry

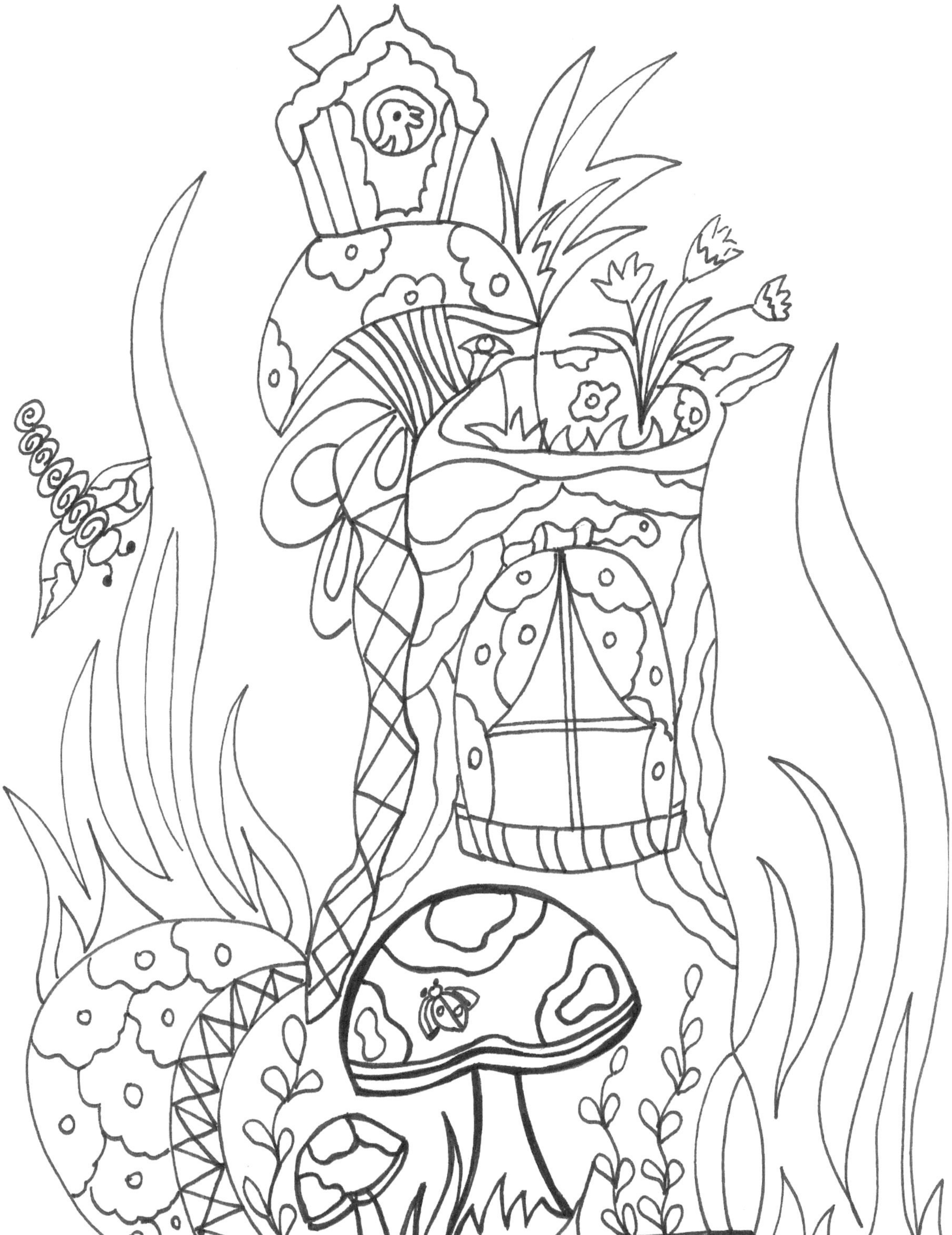

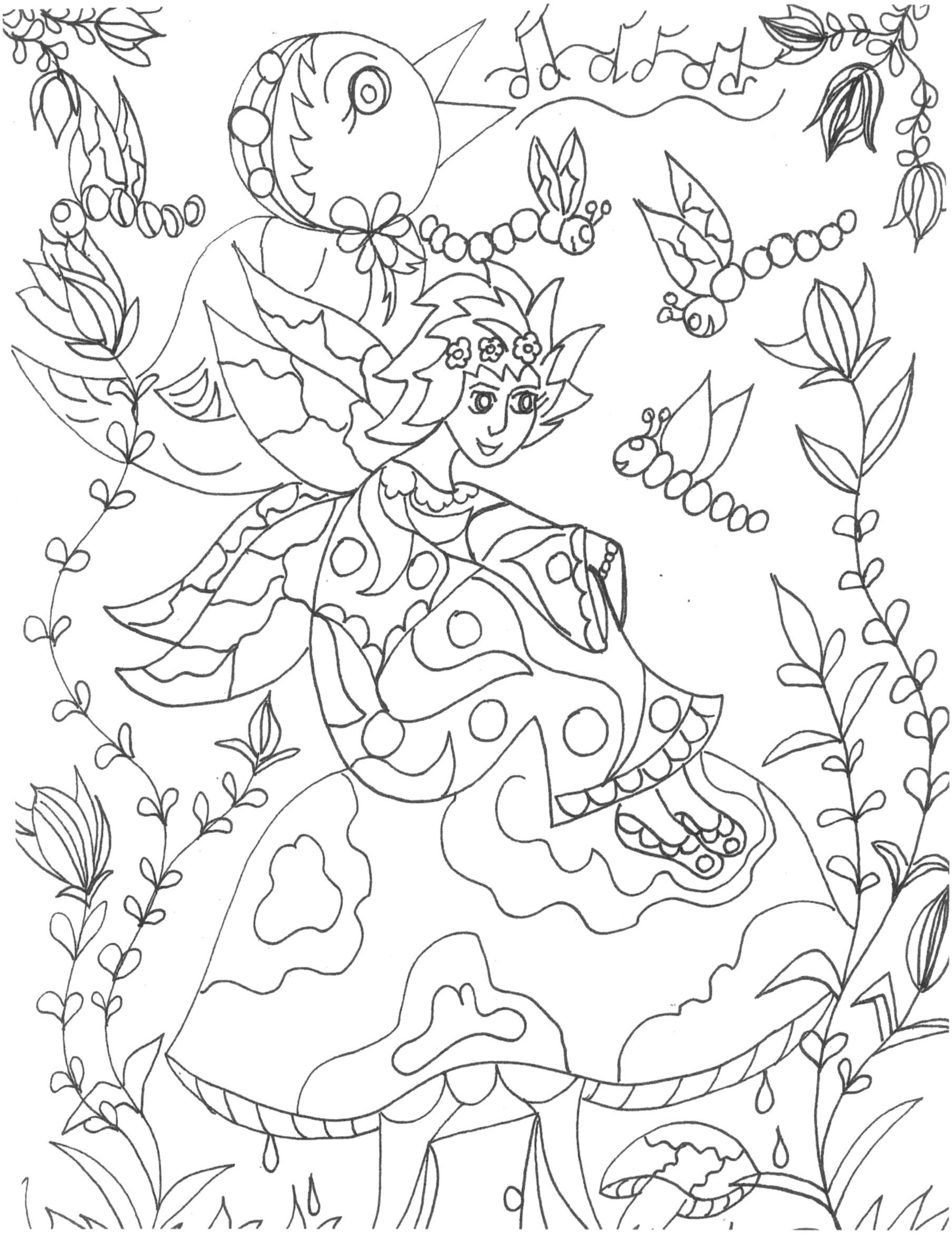

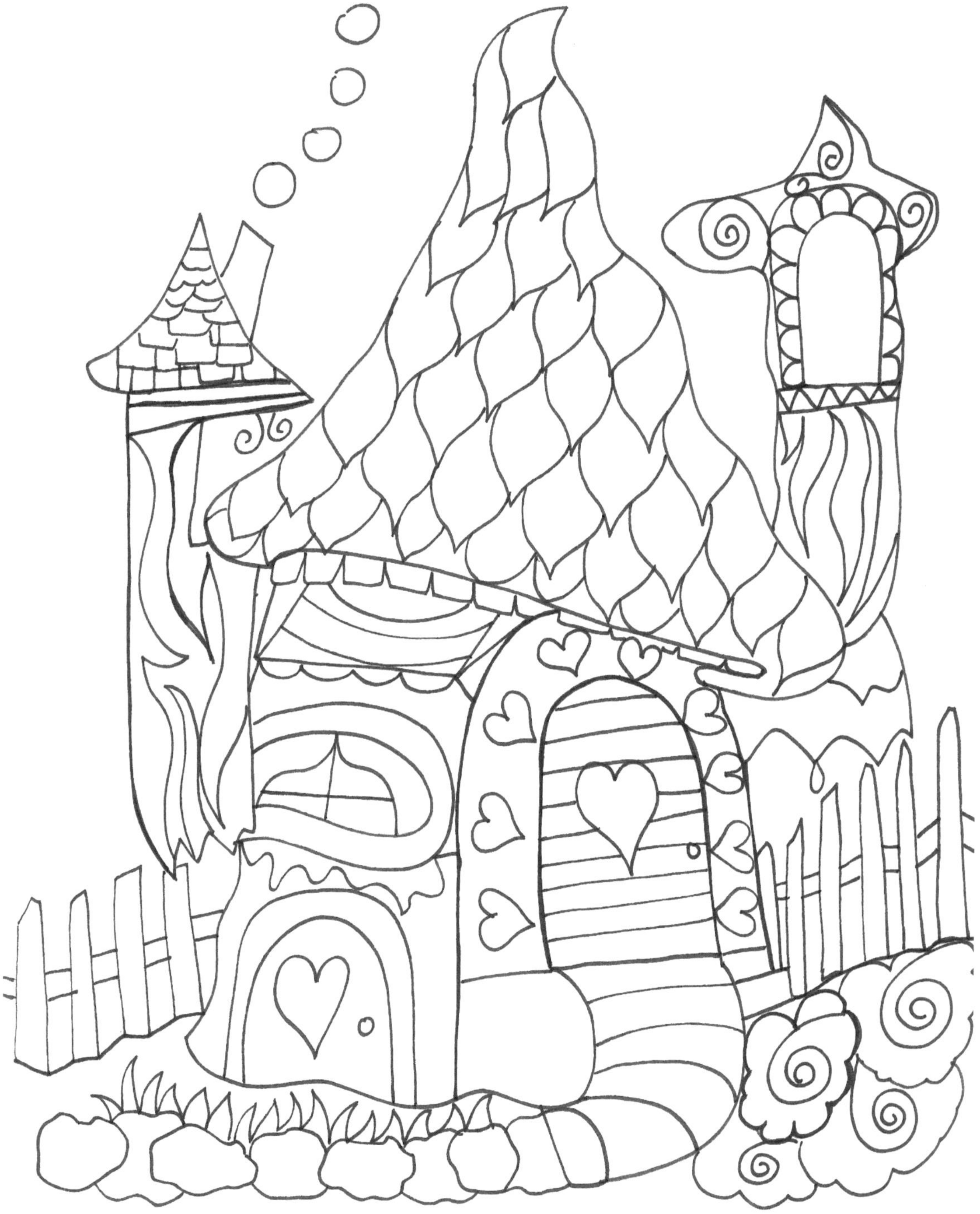

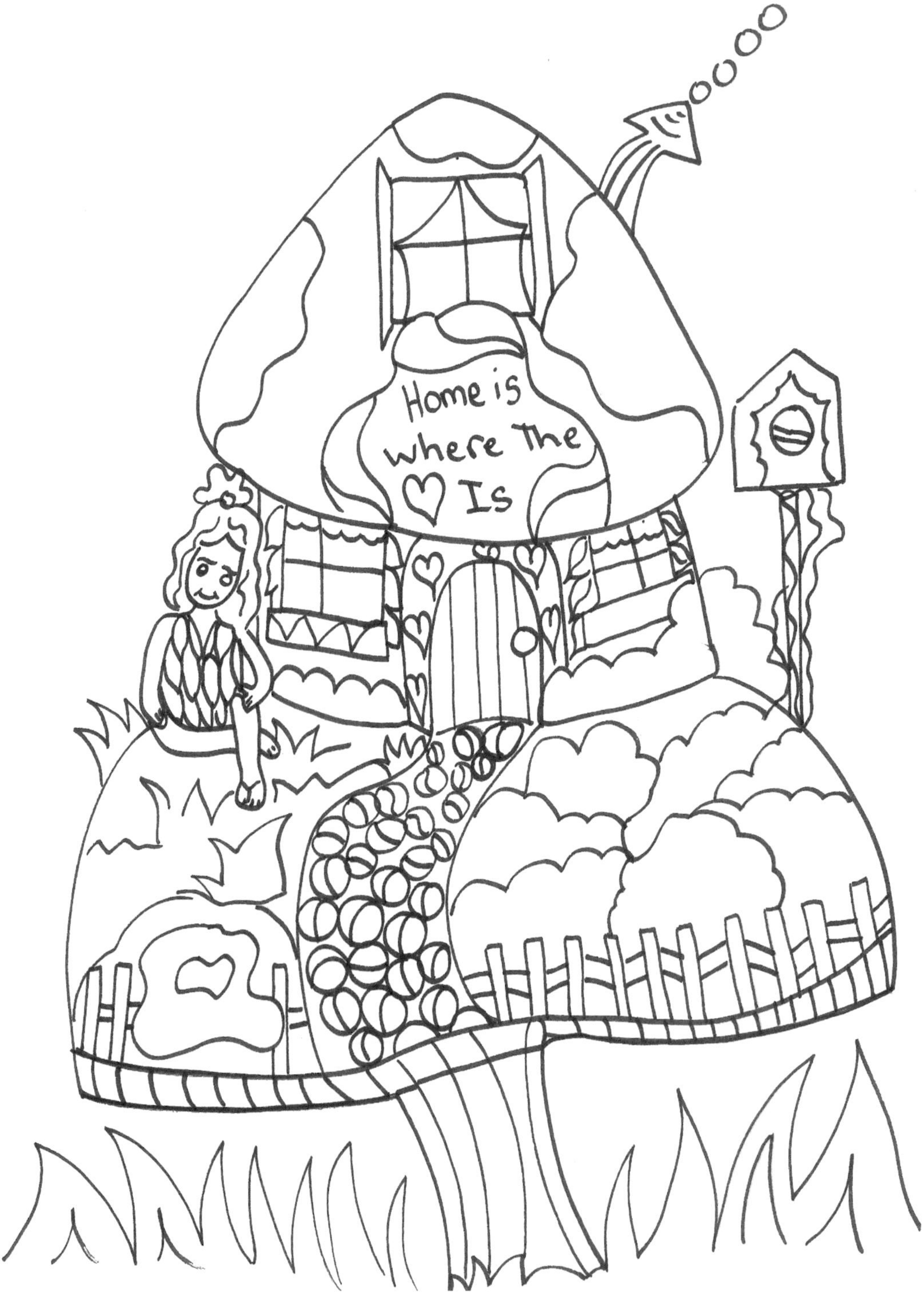
Home is where the ♡ Is

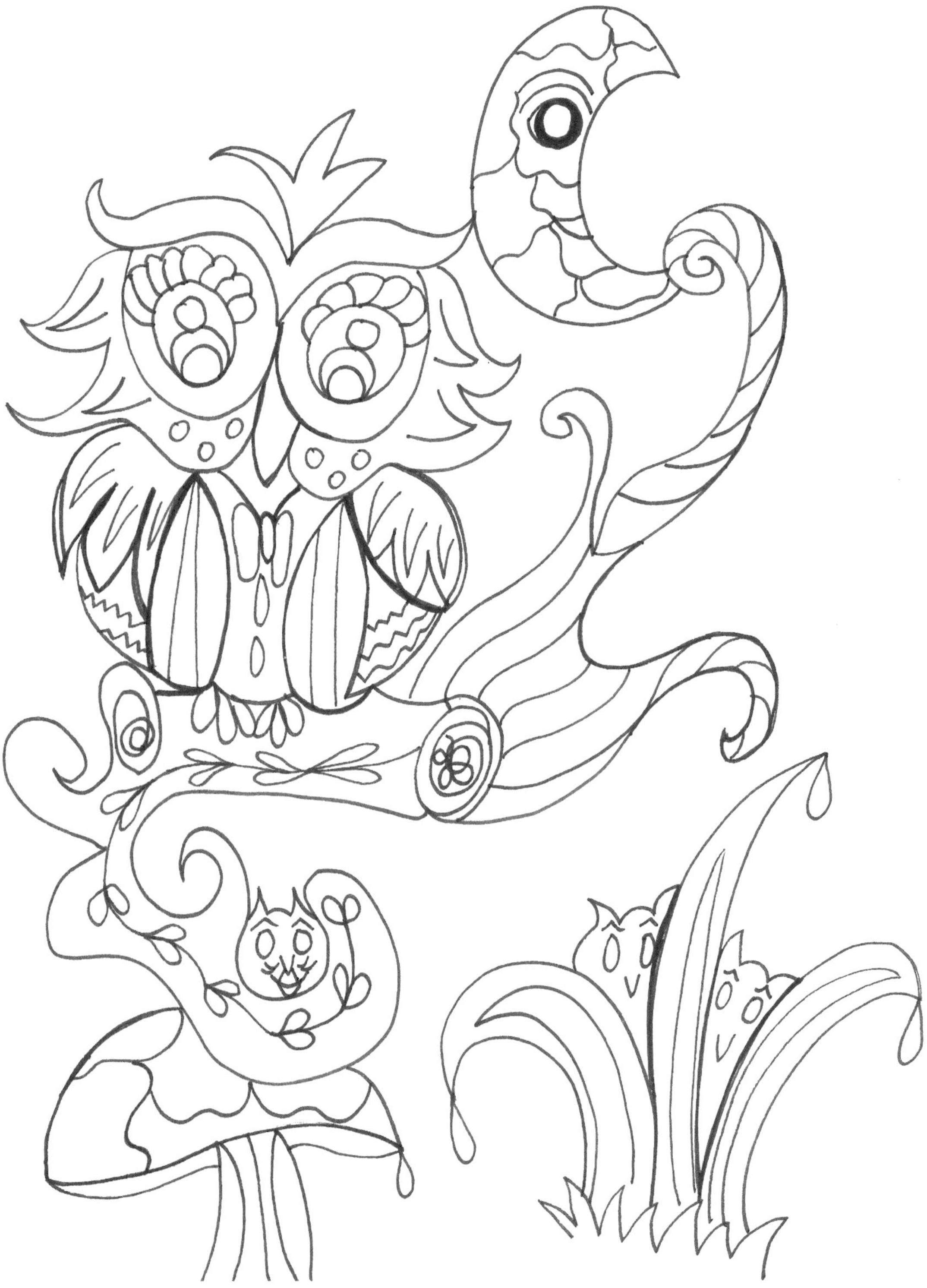

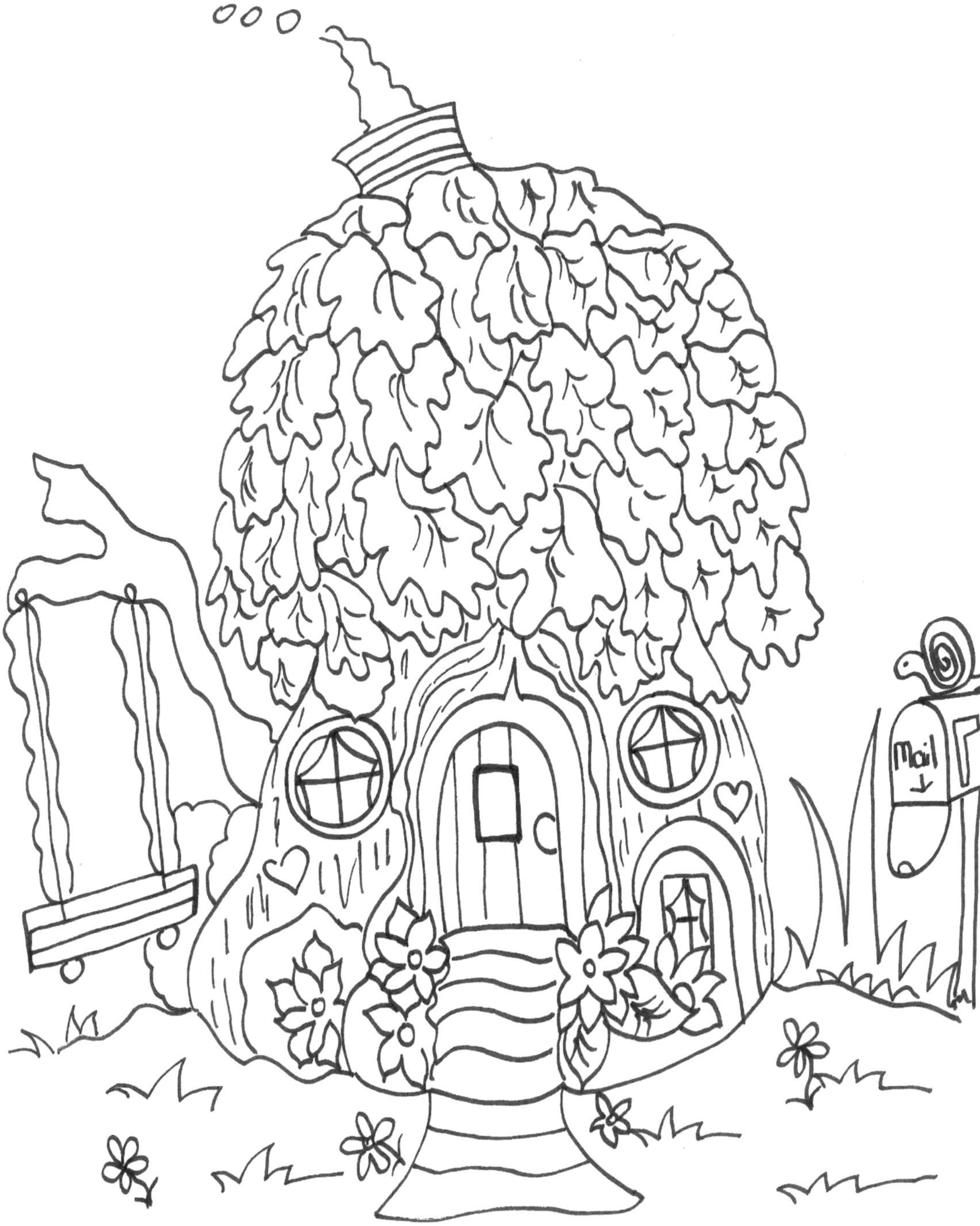
Mail

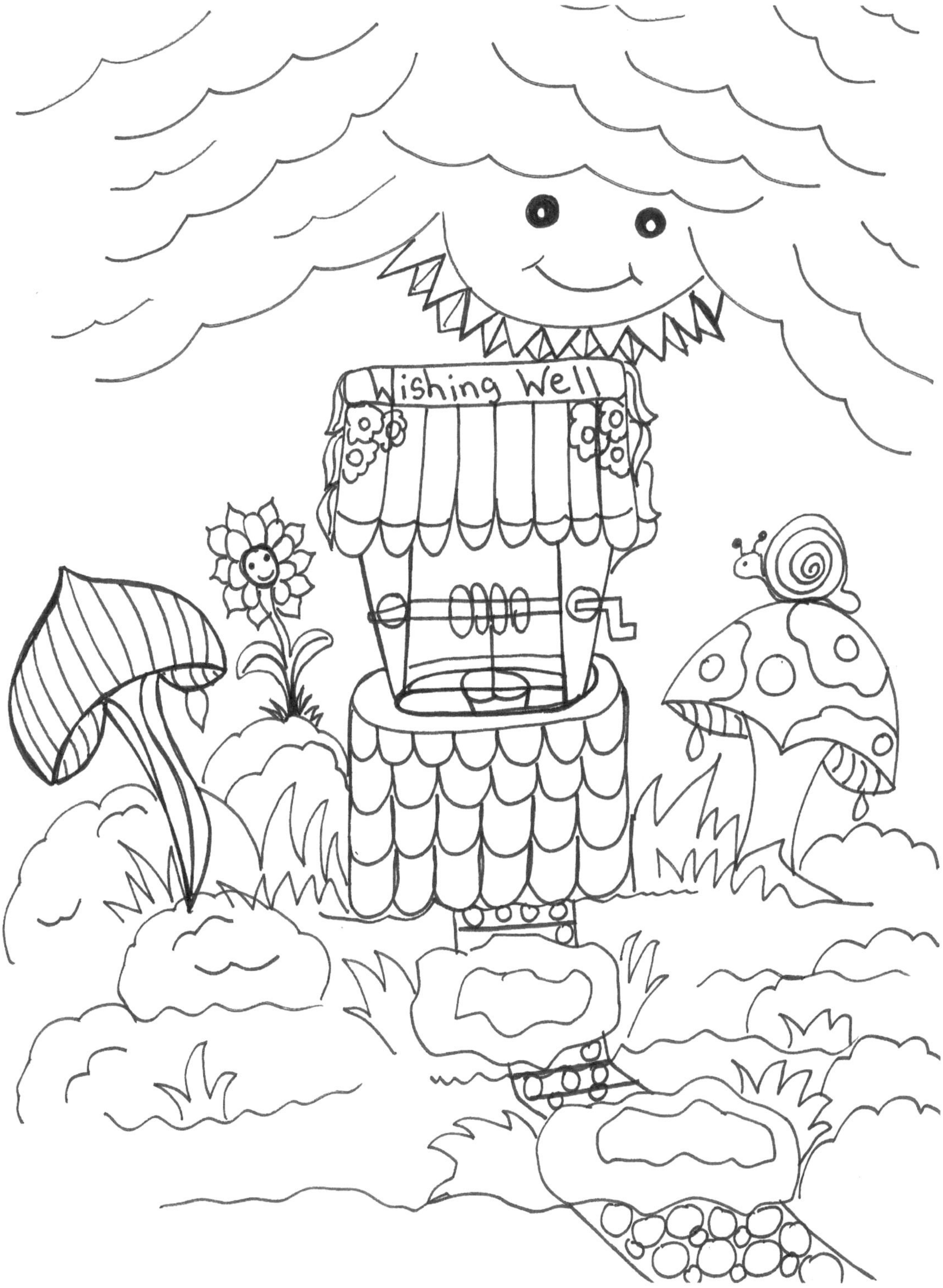
Wishing Well

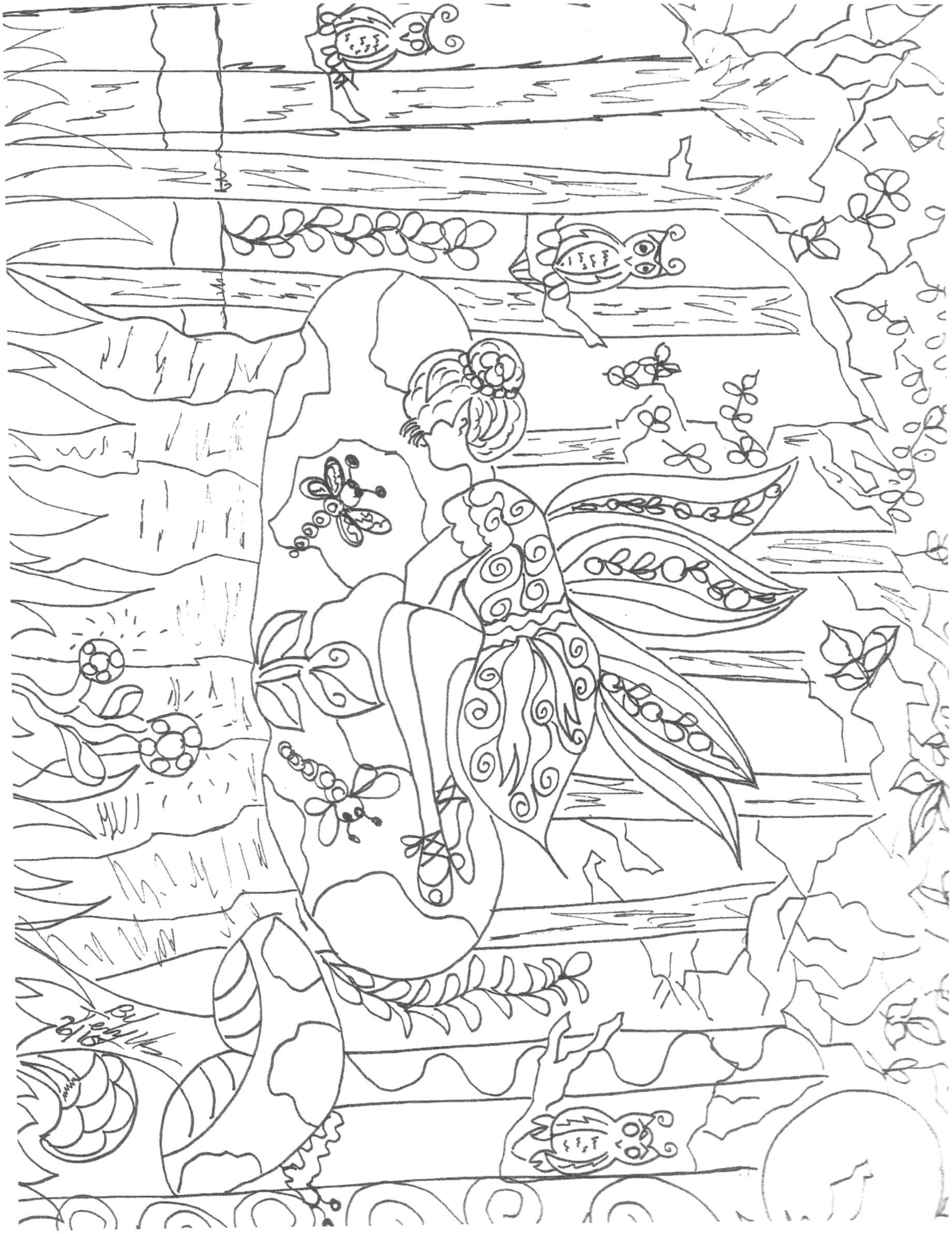

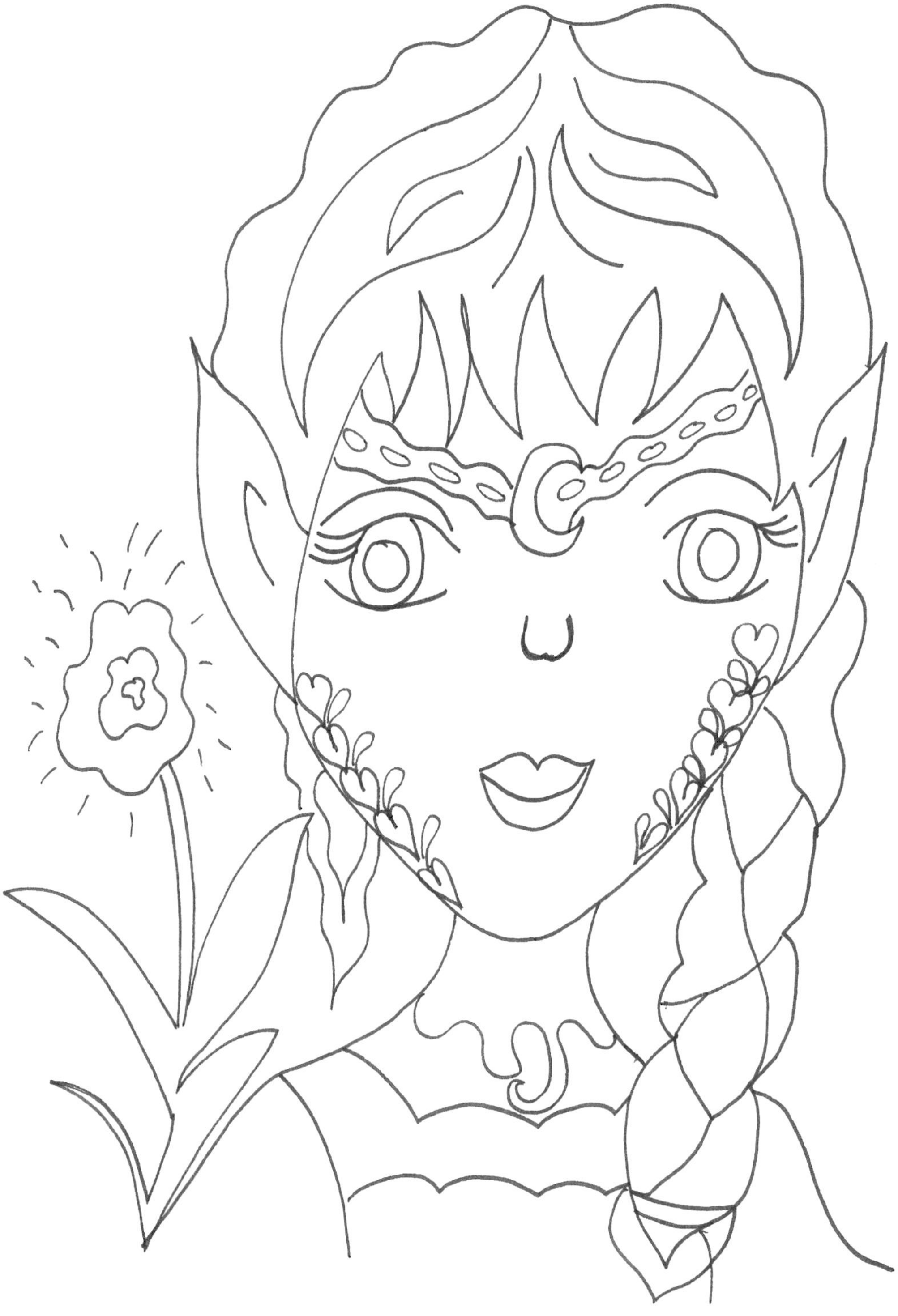

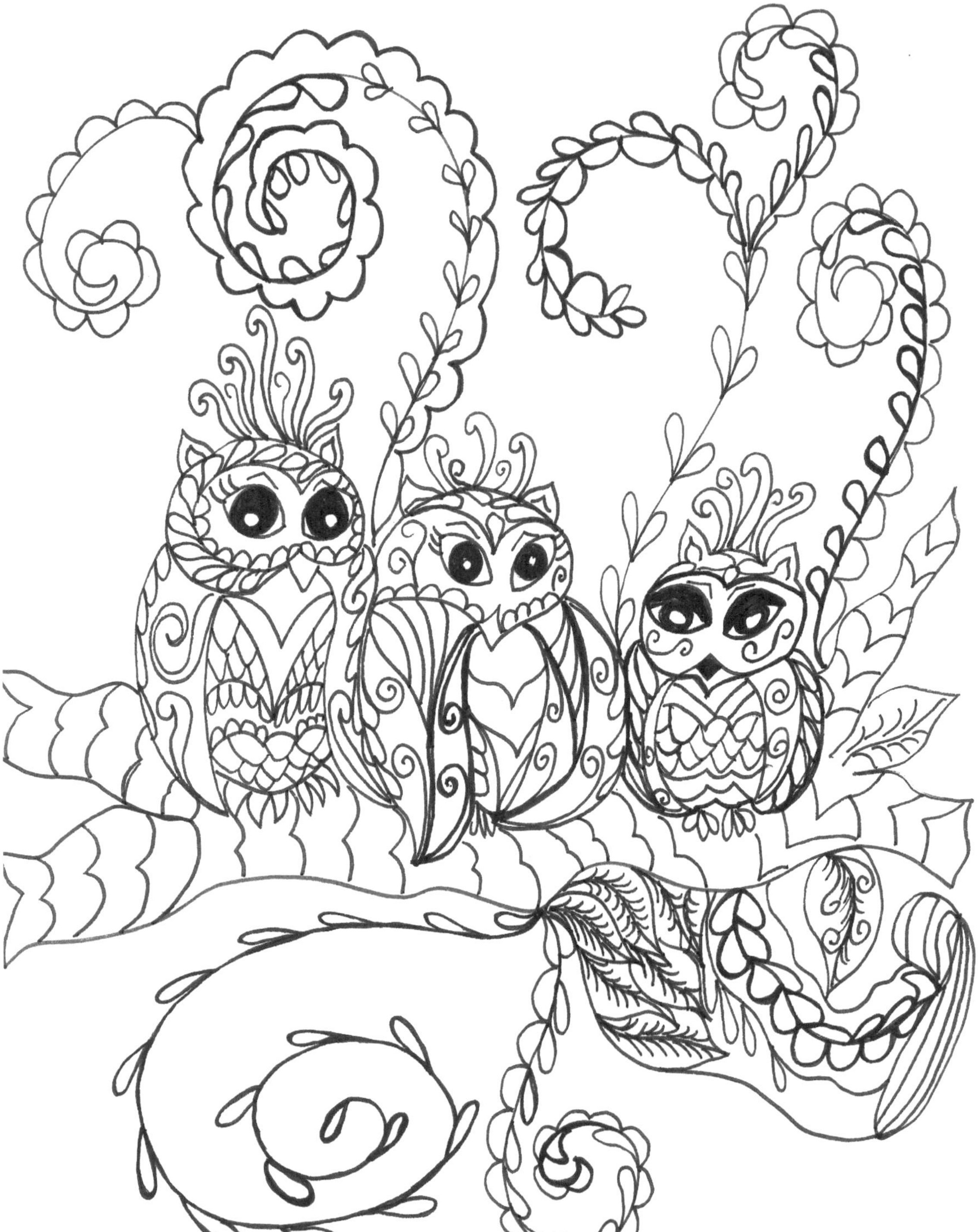

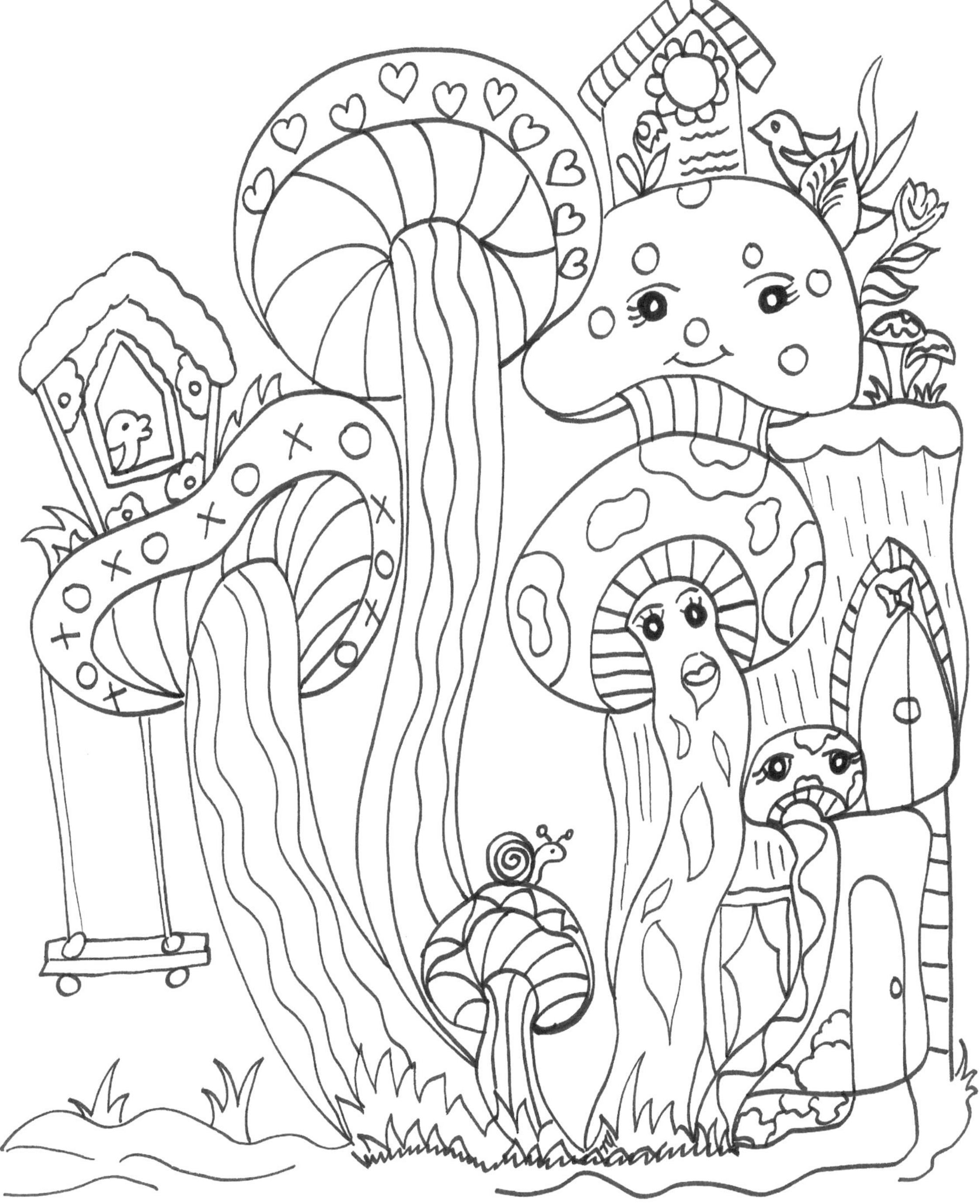

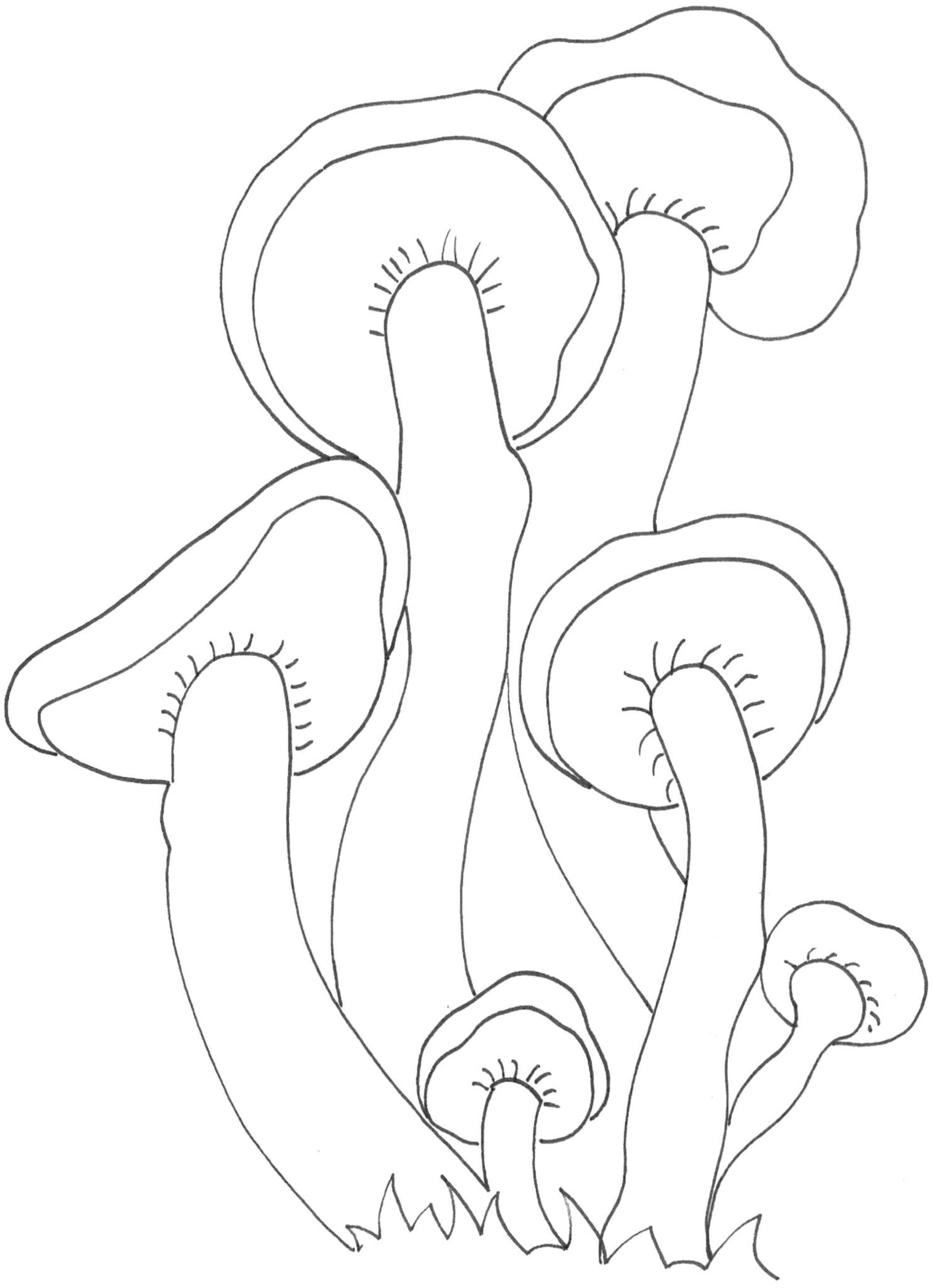

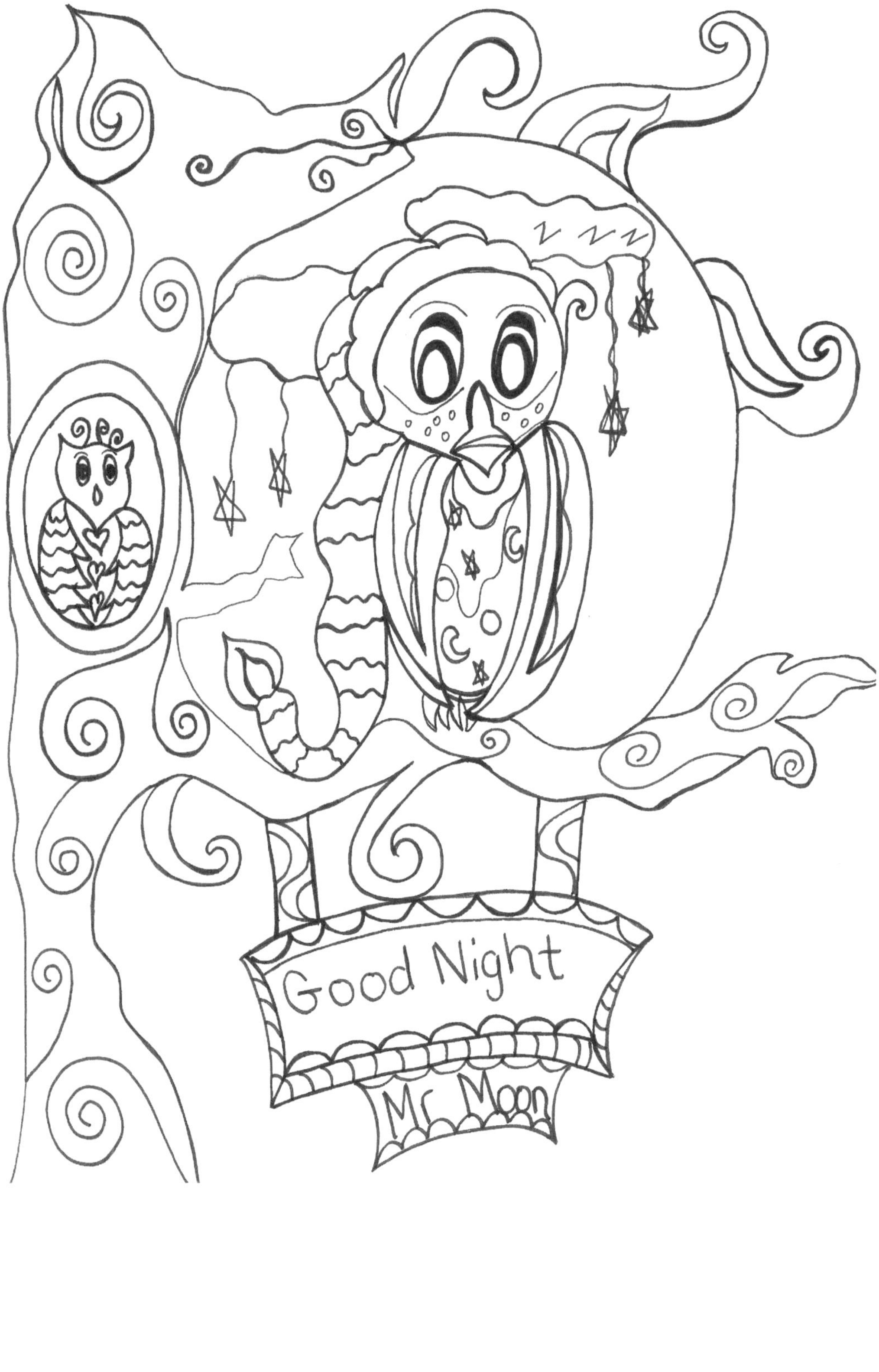
Good Night
Mr Moon

www.ingramcontent.com/pod-product-compliance
Lightning Source LLC
Chambersburg PA
CBHW050429180526
45159CB00005B/2473
* 9 7 8 1 5 1 7 1 3 2 6 7 5 *